To our readers, those students just beginning a life of adventure an

You are braver than you believe, stronger and smarter than you think.

~

A.A. Milne

Sounds of the Night:

A Child's Interactive Book of Fun & Learning

Written & Created by

Brent A. Ford

ISBN 978-1-947348-74-5

www.nviznideas.com

Interactive Components

This version of **Sounds of the Night** combines the best of both worlds. It is a physical book where children can turn the pages, gaze at the photographs and sit close to a parent or loved-one. It is also a book featuring tech-based, interactive components to extend the fun and the learning.

To access the web-based features, use a mobile device (phone or tablet) with nVizn's QR Code Reader. Our app is FREE and does NOT include advertising or in-app purchases. Our system is also designed to be "kid friendly" - meaning that the app does not open up the entire Internet to young children. Our app only reads codes created by us, so users can access only web content that we create and maintain. Look for the nVizn QR Code Reader in your app store.

After downloading the code reader, simply open the app on your phone or tablet, point it at any one of the many codes throughout the book and you are off. The code reader will automatically take you to a webpage for some learning and fun! (You will need an Internet connection to access these features.)

Try it now....open your QR Code reader and point it at this code.

Remember a time outside ... as dusk turned to night.

Remember the soft breeze blowing across your face.

Remember the sounds of a summer evening.

Think back. What did you hear?

Listen now.

Ever wonder about those sounds?

How many different sounds do you hear?

Listen again.

Different animals make those sounds.

Let's learn.

What animal is making this sound?

It is a katydid. Katydids call out
to each other from the tops of trees.

Can you hear the katydids now
within all the nighttime sounds?

What animal is making this sound?

It is a bird called a chuck-will's-widow.
What a funny name for a bird!

Can you hear the chuck-will's-widow now
within all the nighttime sounds?

What animal is making this sound?

Maybe you thought it was a cricket, but it is a cricket frog.

Can you hear the cricket frogs now
within all the nighttime sounds?

What animal is making this sound?

It is a great horned owl. See its horns?
Can you hear the great horned owl now
within all the nighttime sounds?

What animal is making this sound?

It is a cicada – a big green bug with red eyes.
Can you hear the cicadas now within
all the nighttime sounds?

What animal is making this sound?

It is a bullfrog calling out
to other bullfrogs in the pond.

Can you hear the bullfrogs now
within all the nighttime sounds?

What animal is making this sound?

19

It is a bird called a whip-poor-will ...
a bird whose name sounds like its call.

Can you hear the whip-poor-will now
within all the nighttime sounds?

What animal is making this sound?

It is a gray treefrog. Can you hear the gray treefrogs now within all the nighttime sounds?

What animal is making this sound?

It is a red fox calling out to its family.

Can you hear the red fox now within all the nighttime sounds?

What animal is making this sound?

It is a little green treefrog.

Can you hear the green treefrogs now
within all the nighttime sounds?

What animal is making this sound?

Would you believe it ... another frog?
It is a cope's gray treefrog.

Can you hear the cope's gray treefrogs
now within all the nighttime sounds?

What animal is making this sound?

It is a mockingbird. Mockingbirds copy the sounds of other birds, insects and even frogs.

Can you hear the mockingbird now within all the nighttime sounds?

The world is full of magic things patiently waiting ...

.... for our senses to grow sharper.

W.B. Yeats

Now when you listen to the sounds of the night,
what do you hear?

Learn with Simon

Hi, my name is Simon.

Never seen an animal like me? I am an indri (pronounced IN dree) and I live in a place called Madagascar. To learn more about indris and Madagascar, follow this QR code.

I'm nVizn's mascot - the nVizn indri - and I will be your guide as we learn about the world in which we all live. We'll watch a video or two, do an activity or two, and learn to think and work like a scientist. I'll help get you started on a life-long process of learning about how our world works AND why it works as it does.

So, let's get started!

Sounds of the Night

From chirping katydids to croaking frogs and singing birds, our world is filled with the sounds of nature. The variation in the sounds animals make, and how they make those sounds, is truly awe-inspiring.

While there are many different kinds of sounds, we should remember (or learn) that sound is created when something vibrates (moves back and forth really fast). When we yell or sing or hum, there is a part of our body (a part inside our throat) that we make vibrate. How do we know that? Put your hand on your throat....blow out without making a noise. Now put your hand on your throat and sing, hum, yell. Is there a difference? Sure there is...you do not feel anything when you just blow out and you feel something vibrating in your throat when you make a sound. You are causing that vibration, which we hear as singing or yelling or humming. If we can make sound by causing our throats to vibrate, does it make you wonder how other animals make sounds? Follow this QR code to see three different animals - a cricket, a toad and a cicada - and learn how they make sound.

Nature's Thermometer

Crickets are one of the animals we hear calling out to one another at night. Through careful study, scientists learned that crickets chirp more often when it is warmer and less often

when it is colder. By counting the number of chirps in a fixed period of time, we can estimate the temperature. Pretty cool, huh? Follow this QR code to learn more about nature's thermometer - the cricket.

How Big is that Frog?

Frogs create many of the sounds we hear at night and this book features five different frogs and the sounds they make. One thing about looking at pictures of frogs in a book (or on a computer, tablet or phone) is that it can be difficult to know anything about the size of the frog. How big or small are the frogs? Could the frogs we hear on those summer nights actually fit into the palm of your hand like this one? Follow this QR code, and Simon will lead you through an activity to learn about the sizes of these frogs.

Imitation is the sincerest form of flattery.

In the book, we learned that mockingbirds make some of the sounds we hear at night... sounds that are often imitations of other animal sounds. But there is another bird, the lyrebird, that imitates a lot more sounds, including a camera, a car alarm and even a chainsaw. Follow this QR code to see a short video about the lyrebird.

nVizn Ideas

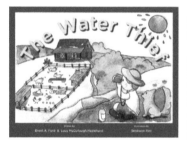

To learn more about these and other children's books that include tech-based resources, follow this QR code.

CPSIA information can be obtained
at www.ICGtesting.com
Printed in the USA
LVHW072251190219
608086LV00020B/104/P